SPEED ZONE
SUPERFAST
CARS

by Alicia Z. Klepeis

po**g**o

Ideas for Parents and Teachers

Pogo Books let children practice reading informational text while introducing them to nonfiction features such as headings, labels, sidebars, maps, and diagrams, as well as a table of contents, glossary, and index.

Carefully leveled text with a strong photo match offers early fluent readers the support they need to succeed.

Before Reading

- "Walk" through the book and point out the various nonfiction features. Ask the student what purpose each feature serves.
- Look at the glossary together. Read and discuss the words.

Read the Book

- Have the child read the book independently.
- Invite him or her to list questions that arise from reading.

After Reading

- Discuss the child's questions. Talk about how he or she might find answers to those questions.
- Prompt the child to think more. Ask: Why can some cars travel so fast? Can you think of any other superfast vehicles?

Pogo Books are published by Jump!
5357 Penn Avenue South
Minneapolis, MN 55419
www.jumplibrary.com

Library of Congress Cataloging-in-Publication Data

Names: Klepeis, Alicia, 1971– author.
Title: Superfast cars / by Alicia Z. Klepeis.
Description: Minneapolis, MN: Jump!, Inc., [2022]
Series: Speed zone | Includes index.
Audience: Ages 7-10
Identifiers: LCCN 2020049990 (print)
LCCN 2020049991 (ebook)
ISBN 9781645279587 (hardcover)
ISBN 9781645279594 (paperback)
ISBN 9781645279600 (ebook)
Subjects: LCSH: Automobiles, Racing–Juvenile literature.
Classification: LCC TL236 .K575 2022 (print)
LCC TL236 (ebook) | DDC 629.228/5–dc23
LC record available at https://lccn.loc.gov/2020049990
LC ebook record available at https://lccn.loc.gov/2020049991

Editor: Eliza Leahy
Designer: Molly Ballanger

Photo Credits: Hafiz Johari/Shutterstock, cover; DigitalStorm/iStock, 1; ZRyzner/Shutterstock, 3; ZUMA/Alamy, 4; Macleoddesigns/Dreamstime, 5; Tkpphotography/Dreamstime, 6-7; Trovoboworod/Shutterstock, 8; Shamleen/Shutterstock, 9; Aleksandr Kondratov/Shutterstock, 10-11, 14-15; mekar/Shutterstock, 12-13; Andrii Kvasov/Shutterstock, 16-17; Raytags/Dreamstime, 18; Leo Mason/Popperfoto/Getty, 19; Max Earey/Shutterstock, 20-21; dimcars/Shutterstock, 23.

Printed in the United States of America at Corporate Graphics in North Mankato, Minnesota.

TABLE OF CONTENTS

CHAPTER 1

START YOUR ENGINES!

Race cars are on the starting line. These long, low cars are dragsters.

dragster ····▶

The cars take off. They can go more than 330 miles (531 kilometers) per hour. That's five times faster than cars on the freeway!

WELCOME TO THE STRIP at LAS VEGAS MOTOR SPEEDWAY
34
TRAXXAS
TOYOTARACING.
GEICO
DODGE
TOYOTA
SUMMIT
GEICO
GOODYEAR

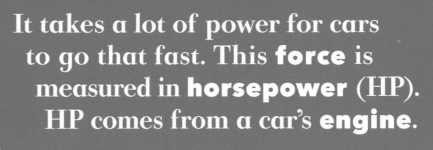

It takes a lot of power for cars to go that fast. This **force** is measured in **horsepower** (HP). HP comes from a car's **engine**.

More HP allows a car to go faster. It also helps a car **accelerate** quickly.

CHAPTER 2

BUILT FOR SPEED

Car engines burn fuel in metal chambers called cylinders. A car with more cylinders burns fuel faster. It goes faster, too.

engine

Most cars have four or six cylinders. Race cars usually have eight or 12. Some of the world's speediest have 16!

cylinder

Turbochargers make cars even faster. They attach to engines. They help engines produce more power. How? They force more air into the cylinders. This burns fuel faster.

DID YOU KNOW?

Sport and race cars often have two turbochargers. They are called twin turbo engines. Some have four. These are called quad turbo engines.

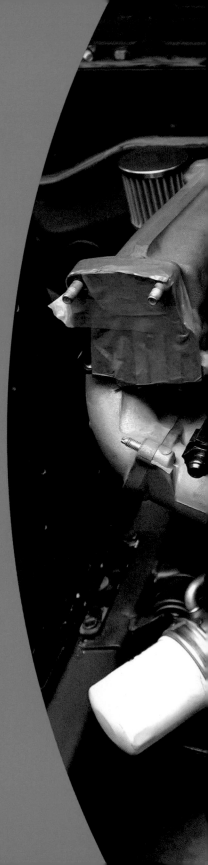

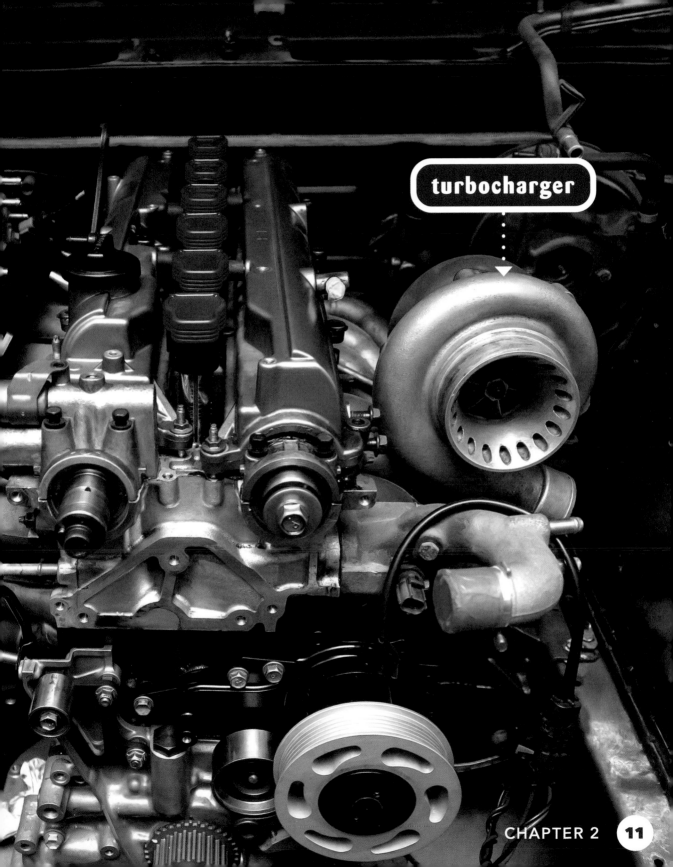

turbocharger

A car's design can help it go faster. **Aerodynamic** features like rear wings and splitters give cars better **traction**.

They redirect airflow. Instead of going under the car, most air flows over it. This presses the car down against the road. This is called **downforce**.

rear wing · · · · ▶

splitter · · · · ▶

TAKE A LOOK!

How do rear wings and splitters give cars better traction? Take a look!

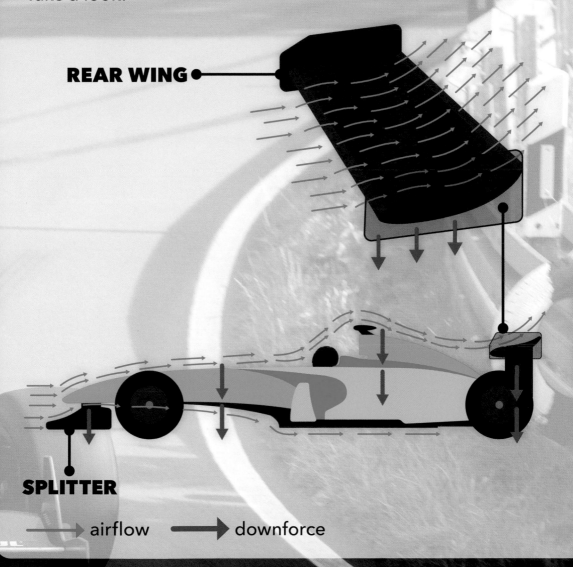

REAR WING

SPLITTER

→ airflow → downforce

Superfast cars often have wide tires. The tires have more rubber than grooves. This gives them more **surface area**. More tire touching the road gives them better traction.

wheel
well

side vent

Superfast cars have other aerodynamic features, too. Many have vents or flaps. Why? These redirect airflow and reduce **drag**. Side vents are one example. They allow air to flow out of the wheel wells.

DID YOU KNOW?

Superfast cars are often made of strong but light materials. One example is **carbon fiber**. This material can improve a car's speed and traction.

CHAPTER 3

TOP SPEEDS

There are many kinds of fast cars. Dragsters accelerate faster than any other car. They can go from 0 to 100 miles (161 km) per hour in less than one second!

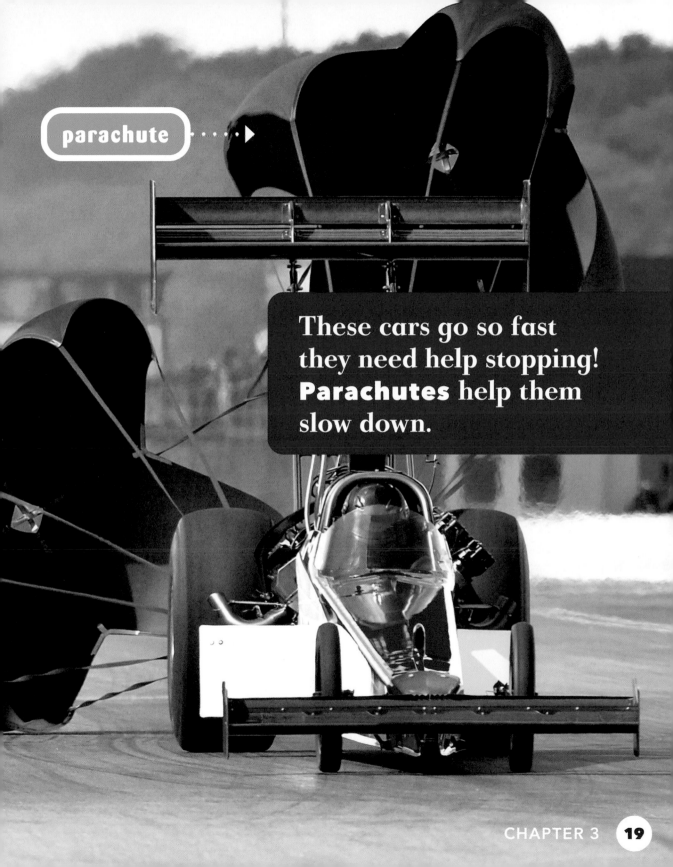

parachute

These cars go so fast they need help stopping! **Parachutes** help them slow down.

Today, several **production cars** can go faster than 250 miles (402 km) per hour. One is the Bugatti Veyron Super Sport. It goes 267 miles (430 km) per hour. The Bugatti Chiron Super Sport goes more than 300 miles (483 km) per hour!

Engineers work to build faster cars. What speeds do you think cars will reach in the future?

DID YOU KNOW?

Companies are working to create greener fast cars. The 2020 Ferrari SF90 Stradale can travel using only **electric power**.

Bugatti Veyron Super Sport

ACTIVITIES & TOOLS

MAKE YOUR OWN RACE CARS

Design two race cars and see which is faster with this fun activity!

What You Need:
- pen or pencil
- paper
- various recycled materials (cardboard, bottles, etc.)
- glue or tape
- scissors

1. Sketch two simple race car designs that you think you could make and would also move quickly.

2. Look around your home and in your recycling bin for materials that you might be able to use to make your race cars. A plastic bottle could work well as a lightweight car body. Straws or wooden skewers may work well as axles.

3. Use the materials you find to construct the cars you sketched.

4. When both cars are ready, line them up on the floor. At the same time, give them a push. Which one moves faster? Why do you think that is? How could you make your faster car even faster?

GLOSSARY

accelerate: To move faster and faster.

aerodynamic: Designed to move through the air easily and quickly.

carbon fiber: A strong, lightweight material that is made up of mainly carbon atoms and is used to make vehicle parts.

downforce: A downward aerodynamic force.

drag: The force that slows motion, action, or advancement.

electric power: Power supplied by or having to do with electricity.

engine: A machine that makes something move by using gasoline, steam, or another energy source.

engineers: People who are specially trained to design and build machines or large structures.

force: Any action that produces, stops, or changes the shape or movement of an object.

horsepower: A unit for measuring the power of an engine.

parachutes: Large pieces of fabric that are attached to thin ropes and spread out in the air to slow whatever is attached to them.

production cars: Cars that are offered for sale to the public.

surface area: The amount of space covering the outside of a 3D object.

traction: The force that keeps a moving body from slipping on a surface.

turbochargers: Devices that force air into engines to create extra power.

INDEX

TO LEARN MORE

Finding more information is as easy as 1, 2, 3.

1 Go to www.factsurfer.com

2 Enter "superfastcars" into the search box.

3 Choose your book to see a list of websites.

FACT SURFER